Knock-Knock!
  Who's there?
Agatha!
  Agatha who?
Agatha sore tooth! It's killing me!

Knock-Knock!
  Who's there?
Albee!
  Albee who?
Albee right back, don't move!

Knock-Knock!
  Who's there?
Alfred!
  Alfred who?
Alfred duh needle if you tie the knot!

Knock-Knock!
  Who's there?
Ali!
  Ali who?
Ali wanna do is dance!

Knock-Knock!
  Who's there?
Alien Don!
  Alien Don who?
Alien Don the wet paint and ruined my shirt!

Knock-Knock!
  Who's there?
Alligator!
  Alligator who?
Alligator for her birthday was a card!

Knock-Knock!
  Who's there?
Alvin!
  Alvin who?
Alvin a nice time on your porch, since you ask!

Knock-Knock!
  Who's there?
Amaso!
  Amaso who?
Amaso sorry you don't remember me!

Ridiculous KNOCK-KNOCKS

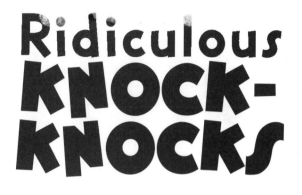

CHRIS TAIT
Illustrated by Mark Zahnd

STERLING

For Franklyn—who makes me ridiculously happy.

Library of Congress Cataloging-in-Publication Available

STERLING and the distinctive Sterling logo are registered trademarks of
Sterling Publishing Co., Inc.

Lot #:
10 9 8 7 6 5 4 3 2 1
09/10
Published by Sterling Publishing Co., Inc.
387 Park Avenue South, New York, NY 10016

© 2001 by Chris Tait

Distributed in Canada by Sterling Publishing
c/o Canadian Manda Group, 165 Dufferin Street
Toronto, Ontario, Canada M6K 3H6
Distributed in Australia by Capricorn Link (Australia) Pty. Ltd.
P.O. Box 704, Windsor, NSW 2756, Australia

Manufactured in Canada

Sterling ISBN 978-1-4027-7852-0

For information about custom editions, special sales, premium and
corporate purchases, please contact Sterling Special Sales
Department at 800-805-5489 or specialsales@sterlingpublishing.com.

Knock-Knock!
Who's there?
Amy!
Amy who?
Amy 'fraid this is the wrong house! I don't know you either.

Knock-Knock!
Who's there?
Aster!
Aster who?
Aster me no questions, I tella you no lies!

Knock-Knock!
Who's there?
Andy!
Andy who?
Andy body home?

Knock-Knock!
Who's there?
Anita!
Anita who?
Anita another knock-knock joke like I need a hole in the head!

Knock-Knock!
  Who's there?
Annie!
  Annie who?
Annie thing I can do for you today?

Knock-Knock!
  Who's there?
Answer!
  Answer who?
Answer all over your porch! It's a mess out here!

Knock-Knock!
  Who's there?
Apple!
  Apple who?
Apple on the door, but nothing happens!

Knock-Knock!
  Who's there?
Arizona!
  Arizona who?
Arizona so many
times I can knock!

Knock-Knock!
  Who's there?
Arnie!
  Arnie who?
Arnie ya even gonna open the door?

Knock-Knock!
  Who's there?
Arnold!
  Arnold who?
Arnold friend from far away!

Knock-Knock!
  Who's there?
Arthur!
  Arthur who?
Arthur any other kind of jokes
you know?

Knock-Knock!
  Who's there?
Asia!
  Asia who?
Asia matter of fact, I
don't remember!

Knock-Knock!
  Who's there?
Astronaut!
  Astronaut who?
Astronaut here, come back later!

7

Knock-Knock!

Who's there?

Avery!

Avery who?

Avery time I come to your house, we go through this!

Knock-Knock!

Who's there?

Axel!

Axel who?

Axel nicely and I might tell ya!

Pretty Please?

Knock-Knock!
  Who's there?
Bacon!
  Bacon who?
Bacon from the heat. It's sweltering out here!

Knock-Knock!
  Who's there?
Baloney!
  Baloney who?
Baloney chase you if you're a matador!

Knock-Knock!
  Who's there?
Bar-B-Q!
  Bar-B-Q who?
Bar-B-Q-t, but I think you're even cuter!

Knock-Knock!
  Who's there?
Barry!
  Barry who?
Barry happy to meet you!

Knock-Knock!
  Who's there?
Bat!
  Bat who?
Bat you can't guess!

Knock-Knock!
  Who's there?
Beaver E.!
  Beaver E. who?
Beaver E. quiet and nobody will find us!

Knock-Knock!
  Who's there?
Becka!
  Becka who?
Becka the bus is the best place to sit!

Knock-Knock!
  Who's there?
Begonia!
  Begonia who?
Begonia bother me!

Knock-Knock!
  Who's there?
Bella!
  Bella who?
Bella bottoms — they're back in style!

Knock-Knock!
  Who's there?
Bellows!
  Bellows who?
Bellows me five bucks and I've come to collect!

Knock-Knock!
  Who's there?
Ben!
  Ben who?
Ben a long time since I've seen you!

Knock-Knock!
  Who's there?
Benny!
  Benny who?
Benny thing happening?

Knock-Knock!
  Who's there?
Beth!
  Beth who?
Beth time for you, stinky!
Peee-uw!

Knock-Knock!
  Who's there?
Betty!
  Betty who?
Betty doesn't even know his own name!

Knock-Knock!
  Who's there?
Bingo!
  Bingo who?
Bingo-ing to this school long?

Knock-Knock!
  Who's there?
Bison!
  Bison who?
Bison girl scout cookies?

Knock-Knock!
  Who's there?
Boo!
  Boo who?
Aw, cheer up, it's not
that bad!

Knock-Knock!
  Who's there?
Boris!
  Boris who?
Boris with another knock-knock joke!

Knock-Knock!
  Who's there?
Bossy!
  Bossy who?
Bossy just fired me!

Knock-Knock!
  Who's there?
Buckle!
  Buckle who?
Buckle get you a soda pop, but not much else!

Knock-Knock!
  Who's there?
Bullet!
  Bullet who?
Bullet all the hay and now he's hungry!

Knock-Knock!
  Who's there?
Bunny!
  Bunny who?
Bunny thing is, I know where the Easter eggs are!

Knock-Knock!
  Who's there?
Burton!
  Burton who?
Burton me are going fishing, want to come?

Knock-Knock!
  Who's there?
Butcher!
  Butcher who?
Butcher shoulder to the door and push!

Knock-Knock!
  Who's there?
Butter!
  Butter who?
Butter stay inside — it looks like rain!

C

Knock-Knock!
  Who's there?
Caesar!
  Caesar who?
Caesar before she fills her squirt gun!

Knock-Knock!
  Who's there?
Candice!
  Candice who?
Candice be love?

Knock-Knock!
  Who's there?
Cannelloni!
  Cannelloni who?
Cannelloni five bucks till next week?

Knock-Knock!
  Who's there?
Canoe!
  Canoe who?
Canoe please open the door?

Knock-Knock!
  Who's there?
Cantelope!
  Cantelope who?
Cantelope, my parents have already planned the
wedding!

Knock-Knock!
  Who's there?
Canter!
  Canter who?
Canter brother come out and play?

Knock-Knock!
  Who's there?
Cargo!
  Cargo who?
Cargo really fast when
you step on the gas!

Knock-Knock!
  Who's there?
Carrie!
  Carrie who?
Carrie this for me, will you, my back's killing me!

Knock-Knock!
  Who's there?
Carrier!
  Carrier who?
Carrier own books, lazybones!

Knock-Knock!
   Who's there?
Carrot!
   Carrot who?
Carrot all for me?

Knock-Knock!
   Who's there?
Cartoon!
   Cartoon who?
Cartoon up just fine, she
purrs like a kitten!

Knock-Knock!
   Who's there?
Catgut!
   Catgut who?
Catgut yer tongue?

Knock-Knock!
   Who's there?
Catsup!
   Catsup who?
Catsup on the roof — want me to go get him?

Knock-Knock!
   Who's there?
Cauliflower!
   Cauliflower who?
Cauliflower by any other name and it's still a daisy!

Will you be my valentine?

Knock-Knock!
 Who's there?
Cecil!
 Cecil who?
Cecil seashells by
the seashore!

Knock-Knock!
 Who's there?
Cello!
 Cello who?
Cello dere, dahling, how ah ya?

Knock-Knock!
 Who's there?
Chair!
 Chair who?
Chair you go again, asking silly questions!

Knock-Knock!
 Who's there?
Checkmate!
 Checkmate who?
Checkmate bounce if you don't put money in the
bank!

Knock-Knock!
 Who's there?
Chester!
 Chester who?
Chester voice from the past!

Knock-Knock!
 Who's there?
Chesterton!
 Chesterton who?
Chesterton of fun!

Knock-Knock!
 Who's there?
Chestnut!
 Chestnut who?
Chestnut easy to open, we need a key!

Knock-Knock!
 Who's there?
Claire!
 Claire who?
Claire the way, I'm coming through!

Knock-Knock!
 Who's there?
Clothesline!
 Clothesline who?
Clothesline all over the floor end up wrinkled!

Knock-Knock!
 Who's there?
Coffin!
 Coffin who?
Coffin that bad means you got a cold!

Knock-Knock!
 Who's there?
Cole!
 Cole who?
Cole me later, I gotta go!

Knock-Knock!
 Who's there?
Colleen!
 Colleen who?
Colleen all cars, Colleen all cars! We have a knock-knock joke in progress!

Knock-Knock!
 Who's there?
Cook!
 Cook who?
You're the one who's cuckoo!

Knock-Knock!
 Who's there?
Cookie!
 Cookie who?
Cookie quit and now I have to make all the food myself!

Knock-Knock!
  Who's there?
Comb!
  Comb who?
Comb on down and I'll tell you!

Knock-Knock!
  Who's there?
Conover.
  Conover who?
Conover remember the punch line!

Knock-Knock!
  Who's there?
Copperfield!
  Copperfield who?
Copperfield bad so I came instead!

That's "whom" not "who."

Knock-Knock!
  Who's there?
Cows go!
  Cows go who?
No, they don't — cows go moo!

Knock-Knock!
  Who's there?
Crewcut!
  Crewcut who?
Crewcut out and I'm the only one left!

Knock-Knock!
  Who's there?
Cupid!
  Cupid who?
Cupid quiet in there!

Knock-Knock!
  Who's there?
Cumin!
  Cumin who?
Cumin side, it's freezing out there!

Knock-Knock!
  Who's there?
Cymbals!
  Cymbals who?
Cymbals have horns and
others don't!

D

Knock-Knock!
Who's there?
Daisy!
  Daisy who?
Daisy like his new school?

Knock-Knock!
  Who's there?
Dancer!
  Dancer who?
Dancer is simple! It's me!

Knock-Knock!
  Who's there?
  Daniella!
    Daniella who?
  Daniella so loud, I
  can hear you just
  fine!

Knock-Knock!
　Who's there?
Darren!
　Darren who?
Darren you to read through to the last page of this knock-knock book!

Knock-Knock!
　Who's there?
Darryl!
　Darryl who?
Darryl never be another girl like you!

Knock-Knock!
　Who's there?
Deena!
　Deena who?
Deena catch a single fish.

24

Knock-Knock!
  Who's there?
Digit!
  Digit who?
Digit least ask her to come with us?

Knock-Knock!
  Who's there?
Dion!
  Dion who?
Dion to play football, let's go!

Knock-Knock!
  Who's there?
Dinosaur!
  Dinosaur who?
Dinosaur, she fell
down playing tennis!

Knock-
Knock!
  Who's
    there?
Disguise!
  Disguise who?
Disguise killing me with these knock-knock jokes!

Knock-Knock!
  Who's there?
Dish wash!
  Dish wash who?
Dish wash my house when I was a little kid!

Knock-Knock!
  Who's there?
Distress!
  Distress who?
Distress is better than that dress!

Knock Knock!
  Who's there?
Don!
  Don who?
Don tell me you don't remember me!

Knock-Knock!
  Who's there?
Don Juan!
  Don Juan who?
Don Juan to go to school today, let's go to the zoo!

Knock-Knock!
  Who's there?
Doughnut!
  Doughnut who?
Doughnut make me reveal my true identity! I'm
under cover!

Knock-Knock!
Who's there?
Dougy!
Dougy who?
Dougy hole in your lawn by accident! Sorry.

Knock-Knock!
Who's there?
Dumbbell!
Dumbbell who?
Dumbbell doesn't work, so I had to knock!

Knock-Knock!
Who's there?
Dunfield!
Dunfield who?
Dunfield good when I woke up this morning!

Knock-Knock!
  Who's there?
Earlier!
  Earlier who?
Earlier fly is undone!

Knock-Knock!
  Who's there?
Eddy!
  Eddy who?
Eddy idea how I can get rid
ub dis cold?

Knock-Knock!
  Who's there?
Eggs!
  Eggs who?
Eggs-actly what I was going to ask you!

Knock-Knock!
  Who's there?
Emma!
  Emma who?
Emma too early for lunch?

Knock-Knock!
  Who's there?
Emma Dunne!
  Emma Dunne who?
Emma Dunne talking to you? I've got better things
to do!

Knock-Knock!
  Who's there?
Emmanuelle!
  Emmanuelle who?
Emmanuelle is what I need to figure out this
intercom!

Knock-Knock!
  Who's there?
Epstein!
  Epstein who?
Epstein some crazy people, but you take the cake!

Knock-Knock!
  Who's there?
Eva!
  Eva who?
Eva going to answer the door?

Knock-Knock!
Who's there?
Evans!
Evans who?
Evans about to open up with rain — let me in!

Knock-Knock!
Who's there?
Everest!
Everest who?
Everest your eyes during class? Teacher thinks
you're sleeping.

Knock-Knock!
Who's there?
Everlast!
Everlast who?
Everlast one of you better come out here!

Knock-Knock!
Who's there?
Eyeball!
Eyeball who?
Eyeball my eyes out every time you go!

Knock-Knock!
  Who's there?
Fajita!
  Fajita who?
Fajita another burrito, I'm gonna be sick!

Knock-Knock!
  Who's there?
Falafel!
  Falafel who?
Falafel my skateboard and landed on my knee!

Knock-Knock!
  Who's there?
Fatso!
  Fatso who?
Fatso funny about all these knock-knock jokes?

Knock-Knock!
  Who's there?
Feline!
  Feline who?
Feline fine, how about you?

Knock-Knock!
  Who's there?
Felix!
  Felix who?
Felix me again, I'm not gonna pet your dog anymore!

Knock-Knock!
  Who's there?
Ferdinand!
  Ferdinand who?
Ferdinand beats two in the bush!

Knock-Knock!
  Who's there?
Ferris!
  Ferris who?
Ferris fair, you win!

Knock-Knock!
  Who's there?
Fiddle!
  Fiddle who?
Fiddle make you happy, I'll tell you!

Knock-Knock!
  Who's there?
Fido!
  Fido who?
Fi don't come inside, I'm gonna freeze!

Knock-Knock!
  Who's there?
Fish!
  Fish who?
Fish-us temper your dog's got! He should be on a
leash!

Knock-Knock!
    Who's there?
      Fission!
        Fission who?
        Fission a bowl are safe
            from the cat!

Knock-Knock!
  Who's there?
Fizzle!
  Fizzle who?
Fizzle make ya burp!

Knock-Knock!
  Who's there?
Fletcher!
  Fletcher who?
Fletcher door open just a crack, I'll slip this pizza inside!

Knock-Knock!
  Who's there?
Flounder!
  Flounder who?
Flounder key on the lawn — ya want it back?

Knock-Knock!
  Who's there?
Fossil!
  Fossil who?
Fossil last time, open the door!

Knock-Knock!
  Who's there?
Francis!
  Francis who?
Francis between Spain and Germany.

Knock-Knock!
  Who's there?
Frankie!
  Frankie who?
Frankie my dear, I don't give a darn!

Knock-Knock!
  Who's there?
Freda!
  Freda who?
Freda make knock-knock jokes all day long!

Knock-Knock!
  Who's there?
Freddie!
  Freddie who?
Freddie cat, why don't you come
out here and find out!

Knock-Knock!
  Who's there?
Fredo!
  Fredo who?
Fredo the dark, turn on the
porch light!

Knock-Knock!
  Who's there?
Fred N. Green!
  Fred N. Green who?
Fred N. Green are my favorite colors!

Knock-Knock!
  Who's there?
Furlong!
  Furlong who?
Furlong time I wanted to come by and say hi!

Knock-Knock!
  Who's there?
Fuschia!
  Fuschia who?
Fuschia ever call me, I'm going to be out!

Knock-Knock!
  Who's there?
Fuzzy!
  Fuzzy who?
Fuzzy sake of old times, open the door!

Knock-Knock!
  Who's there?
Gabe!
  Gabe who?
Gabe it my best shot and that's all I can do!

Knock-Knock!
  Who's there?
George!
  George who?
George-us lady, give me a kiss!

Knock-Knock!
  Who's there?
Gino!
  Gino who?
Gino who it is, I'm your twin brother!

Knock-Knock!
  Who's there?
Giovanni!
  Giovanni who?
Giovanni go to the park with me?

Knock-Knock!
  Who's there?
Gladys!
  Gladys who?
Gladys finally summer vacation, aren't you?

Knock-Knock!
  Who's there?
Gladiola!
  Gladiola who?
Gladiola door open for me!

Knock-Knock!
  Who's there?
Gopher!
  Gopher who?
Gopher crying out loud,
stop asking!

Knock-Knock!
  Who's there?
Gorilla!
  Gorilla who?
Gorilla cheese is good with ketchup!

Knock-Knock!
  Who's there?
Grape!
  Grape who?
Grape game the other day, you're still the champ!

Knock-Knock!
  Who's there?
Greta!
  Greta who?
Greta phone and then I can stop knocking!

Knock-Knock!
  Who's there?
Guitar!
  Guitar who?
Guitar gloves and let's make a snowman!

Knock-Knock!
  Who's there?
Gunga din.
  Gunga din who?
I gunga din! That's why I'm knock-
ing on the door, goofy!

Knock-Knock!
  Who's there?
Gustavo!
  Gustavo who?
Gustavo very good idea!

Knock-Knock!
   Who's there?
Hairdo!
   Hairdo who?
Hairdo some crazy stuff,
lend me your comb!

Knock-Knock!
   Who's there?
Hansel!
   Hansel who?
Hansel freeze right off if
you don't let me in!

Knock-Knock!
   Who's there?
Hardy!
   Hardy who?
Hardy recognized you without
your glasses!

Knock-Knock!
   Who's there?
Hayden!
   Hayden who?
Hayden won't do any good — I can see you through the mail slot!

Knock-Knock!
   Who's there?
Heavy!
   Heavy who?
Heavy ever been to
sea, Billy?

Knock-Knock!
   Who's there?
Heidi!
   Heidi who?
Heidi claire,
something
smells delicious!

Knock-Knock!
   Who's there?
Heifer!
   Heifer who?
Heifer heard so many knock-knock jokes?

Knock-Knock!
  Who's there?
Hi!
  Hi who?
Hi who, hi who, it's off to work we go!

Knock-Knock!
  Who's there?
Hockey!
  Hockey who?
Hockey doesn't work, so I had to knock!

Knock-Knock!
  Who's there?
Hole!
  Hole who?
Hole-he cow, Batman, time to head back to the cave!

Knock-Knock!
  Who's there?
Homer!
  Homer who?
Homer 'gain after a long day of school. Time for fun!

Knock-Knock!
  Who's there?
House!
  House who?
House about you let me come inside!

Knock-Knock!
Who's there?
Howell!
Howell who?
Howell you ever make friends if you stay locked up
like that?

Knock-Knock!
Who's there?
Hugh!
Hugh who?
Yes, can I help you?

Knock-Knock!
Who's there?
Hugo!
Hugo who?
Hugo on and on about these knock-knock jokes!

Knock-Knock!
Who's there?
Hutch!
Hutch who?
You sound like
you're coming
down with
something!

Knock-Knock!
 Who's there?
Icy!
 Icy who?
Icy you in there, let me in!

Knock-Knock!
 Who's there?
Ida!
 Ida who?
Ida brought my home-
work if my dog hadn't
eaten it!

Knock-Knock!
 Who's there?
Iguana!
 Iguana who?
Iguana sell you these great magazines!

Knock-Knock!
    Who's there?
India!
    India who?
India afternoon, I'm going to the dentist!

Knock-Knock!
    Who's there?
Innuendo!
    Innuendo who?
Innuendo the dinner you get dessert.

Knock-Knock!
    Who's there?
Interrupting cow!
    Interrupting (*say* "Mooooooooooooo!" *as the other person is saying* "Interrupting Cow who?") cow who?

Knock-Knock!
    Who's there!
Irish!
    Irish who?
Irish you'd take me away from all this!

Knock-Knock!
    Who's there?
Isabella!
    Isabella who?
Isabella broken or what? I've been ringing forever!

Knock-Knock!
Who's there?
Isaiah!
Isaiah who?
Isaiah nothing else until you let me in!

Knock-Knock!
Who's there?
Island!
Island who?
Island on your doorstep and you don't let me in— just my luck!

Knock-Knock!
Who's there?
Issue!
Issue who?
Issue blind? It's me!

Knock-Knock!
Who's there?
Ivana!
Ivana who?
Ivana go to the movie, you vanna buy me a ticket?

Knock-Knock!
  Who's there?
Jason!
  Jason who?
Jason your brother will only get you in trouble!

Knock-Knock!
  Who's there?
Jerry.
  Jerry who?
Jerry funny, you know darn well who it is!

Knock-Knock!
  Who's there?
Jess!
  Jess who?
Hey, that's my line!

Knock-Knock!
  Who's there?
Jilly!
  Jilly who?
Jilly out here, but I bet it's warm in there!

Knock-Knock!
  Who's there?
Jimmy!
  Jimmy who?
Jimmy back my book, you
thief!

Knock-Knock!
  Who's there?
Jiminy!
  Jiminy who?
Jiminy were at the park playing baseball.

Knock-Knock!
  Who's there?
Jo!
  Jo who?
Jo, team, Jo!

Knock-Knock!
  Who's there?
Joanna!
  Joanna who?
Joanna big kiss or what?

Knock-Knock!
  Who's there?
Joey!
  Joey who?
Joey to the world! It's Christmas!

Knock-Knock!
Who's there?
Juan!
Juan who?
Juan to go for a pizza?

Knock-Knock!
Who's there?
Juanita!
Juanita who?
Juanita sandwich with me?

Knock-Knock!
Who's there?
Juliet.
Juliet who?
Juliet all the pizza and there ain't none left
for me, Pa!

Knock-Knock!
Who's there?
Julius!
Julius who?
Julius just jealous
that you know all the
good jokes!

K

Knock-Knock!
  Who's there?
Kansas!
  Kansas who?
Kansas what tuna come in, silly!

Knock-Knock!
  Who's there?
Kenneth!
  Kenneth who?
Kenneth little kids come inthide?

Knock-Knock!
  Who's there?
Kenny!
  Kenny who?
Kenny let me in or what?

Knock-Knock!
  Who's there?
Kenya.
  Kenya who?
Kenya fix the doorbell — I've been knocking for
hours!

Knock-Knock!
  Who's there?
Kerry!
  Kerry who?
Kerry me upstairs, would you? I'm
pooped!

Knock-Knock!
  Who's there?
Ketchup!
  Ketchup who?
Ketchup on your
homework!

Knock-Knock!
  Who's there?
Kitten!
  Kitten who?
Kitten the park hit me with a frisbee!

Knock-Knock!
  Who's there?
Klaus!
  Klaus who?
Klaus the window, I can hear your television all the
way down the street!

Knock-Knock!
  Who's there?
Kumquat!
  Kumquat who?
Kumquat may, we'll always be friends!

Knock-Knock!
Who's there?
L.A.!
L.A. who?
L.A. down to take a nap and slept right through dinner!

Knock-Knock!
Who's there?
Lego!
Lego who?
Lego of me and I'll tell you!

Knock-Knock!
Who's there?
Leif!
Leif who?
Leif me alone with all your silly questions!

Knock-Knock!
  Who's there?
Lena!
  Lena who?
Lena little closer and maybe I'll tell you!

Knock-Knock!
  Who's there?
Lettuce!
  Lettuce who?
Lettuce in or we'll huff and we'll puff and we'll blow
the house down!

Knock-Knock!
  Who's there?
Lion!
  Lion who?
Lion down on the job will get you fired!

Knock-Knock!
  Who's there?
Lisa!
  Lisa who?
Lisa you can do is let me in! It's
pouring rain!

Knock-Knock!
  Who's there?
Little old lady!
  Little old lady who?
Do you sing opera too?

Knock-Knock!
  Who's there?
Liza!
  Liza who?
Liza only gonna get you into trouble, buster!

Knock-Knock!
  Who's there?
Lotta!
  Lotta who?
Lotta knock-knocks for such a little book!

Knock-Knock!
  Who's there?
Lucille!
  Lucille who?
Lucille me out here — just let me
in!

Knock-Knock!
  Who's there?
Luncheon!
  Luncheon who?
Luncheon candy
and snacks and
you'll get sick!

M

Knock-Knock!
  Who's there?
Mabel!
  Mabel who?
Mabel syrup is great
on waffles!

Knock-Knock!
  Who's there?
Manny!
  Manny who?
Manny people
ask me that question. I wonder why?

Knock-Knock!
  Who's there?
Maria!
  Maria who?
Maria me, I love you!

Knock-Knock!
  Who's there?
Maple!
  Maple who?
Maple the door off
the hinges if you
don't let me in!

Don't make
me pull that
thing down!

Knock-Knock!
  Who's there?
Markus!
  Markus who?
Markus down for
two tickets, we're
going to the show!

Knock-Knock!
  Who's there?
Marshall!
  Marshall who?
Marshall get you covered in mud!

Knock-Knock!
  Who's there?
Max!
  Max who?
Max no difference how long it takes — I've got all
day!

Knock-Knock!
  Who's there?
Maya!
  Maya who?
Maya foot seems to be caught in your door!

Knock-Knock!
  Who's there?
Matthew!
  Matthew who?
Matthew need help with. Science you might be better at!

Knock-Knock!
  Who's there?
Mercedes!
  Mercedes who?
Mercedes your best friend.

Knock-Knock!
  Who's there?
Meter!
  Meter who?
Meter at the train station at 7 o'clock sharp!

Knock-Knock!
  Who's there?
Mice!
  Mice who?
Mice to make your acquaintance!

Knock-Knock!
　Who's there?
Micro!
　Micro who?
Micro is missing — is your crow around?

Knock-Knock!
　Who's there?
Mistake!
　Mistake who?
Mistake aspirin if you have a headache!

Knock-Knock!
　Who's there?
Mister!
　Mister who?
Mister last joke, get her to tell it again!

Knock-Knock!
  Who's there?
Mission!
  Mission who?
Mission you is making me sad, come home!

Knock-Knock!
  Who's there?
Modem!
  Modem who?
Modem lawns, the grass is getting long!

Knock-Knock!
  Who's there?
Morris!
  Morris who?
Morris code didn't work, so I had to come tell ya in person!

Knock-Knock!
  Who's there?
Morrie!
  Morrie who?
Morrie tries to kiss me the more I run away!

Knock-Knock!
  Who's there?
Moscow!
  Moscow who?
Moscow moos but Pa's is very quiet!

Knock-Knock!
  Who's there?
Moustache!
  Moustache who?
Moustache you a question, you ready?

Knock-Knock!
  Who's there?
Mustard!
  Mustard who?
Mustard heard this one before!

N

Who's there?

Knock-Knock!
  Who's there?
Noah!
  Noah who?
Noah don't recognize
your voice either!

Knock-Knock!
  Who's there?
Nunio!
  Nunio who?
Nunio wanna open the door?

Knock-Knock!
 Who's there?
Obi wan!
 Obi wan who?
Obi wan of the good guys and let me in!

Knock-Knock!
 Who's there?
Oil change!
 Oil change who?
Oil change my clothes
 and come back later!

Knock-Knock!
 Who's there?
Olive!
 Olive who?
Olive the times I've been to your house and you still
don't know me?

Knock-Knock!
 Who's there?
Oliver!
 Oliver who?
Oliver clothes are getting soaked, it's pouring out here!

Knock-Knock!
 Who's there?
Ollie!
 Ollie who?
Ollie want is to come inside.

Knock-Knock!
 Who's there?
Ooze!
 Ooze who?
Ooze the boss around here anyway?

Knock-Knock!
 Who's there?
Orange!
 Orange who?
Orange you gonna let me in?

Knock-Knock!
 Who's there?
Orange juice!
 Orange juice who?
Orange juice the guy I just talked to?

Knock-Knock!
  Who's there?
Otis!
  Otis who?
Otis a lie — say 'tis a lie!

Knock-Knock!
  Who's there?
Otto!
  Otto who?
Otto be asleep by now!

Knock-Knock!
  Who's there?
Owl!
  Owl who?
Owl call ya later!

Knock-Knock!
  Who's there?
Paris!
    Paris who?
Paris good but apple is better!

Knock-Knock!
  Who's there?
Pasta!
    Pasta who?
Pasta gravy please!

Knock-Knock!
  Who's there?
Pencil!
    Pencil who?
Pencil keep your legs warm!

Knock-Knock!
  Who's there?
Pecan!
  Pecan who?
Pecan the closet, there's a surprise for you!

Knock-Knock!
  Who's there?
Pepper!
  Pepper who?
Pepper up for the cheerleading rally!

Knock-Knock!
  Who's there?
Pepperoni!
  Pepperoni who?
Pepperoni makes me sneeze!

Knock-Knock!
  Who's there?
Personal!
  Personal who?
Personal catch their death of cold out here!

Knock-Knock!
  Who's there?
Petunia!
  Petunia who?
Petunia and me, there's only a door!

Knock-Knock!
 Who's there?
Philip!
 Philip who?
Philip my gas tank, will you?

Knock-Knock!
 Who's there?
Pickle!
 Pickle who?
Pickle little flower and give it to your mother!

Knock-Knock!
 Who's there?
Pierre!
 Pierre who?
Pierre at five o'clock and you'll find out!

Knock-Knock!
 Who's there?
Pigment!
 Pigment who?
Pigment a lot to me,
have you seen him?

Knock-Knock!
  Who's there?
Piña!
  Piña who?
Piña long time since I've seen you!

Knock-Knock!
  Who's there?
Pinafore.
  Pinafore who?
Pinafore your thoughts!

Knock-Knock!
  Who's there?
Pizza!
  Pizza who?
Pizza my coat is caught in the door!

Knock-Knock!
  Who's there?
Plane!
  Plane who?
Plane dumb won't help you now!

Knock-Knock!
  Who's there?
Poker!
  Poker who?
Poker and she'll get real mad!

Knock-Knock!
  Who's there?
Police!
  Police who?
Police let me in, it's cold out here!

Knock-Knock!
  Who's there?
Porpoise!
  Porpoise who?
Porpoise of my visit is an unpaid bill!

Knock-Knock!
  Who's there?
Puck!
  Puck who?
Puck-er up, I'm gonna kiss you!

Knock-Knock!
  Who's there?
Pumpkin!
  Pumpkin who?
Pumpkin get ya water!

Knock-Knock!
  Who's there?
Pylon!
  Pylon who?
Pylon the knock-knocks, I love 'em!

Knock-Knock!
 Who's there?
Rabbit!
 Rabbit who?
Rabbit around your head
like a turban!

Knock-Knock!
 Who's there?
Rain!
 Rain who?
Rain dear, you remember
me, the one with the
shiny nose?

Knock-Knock!
 Who's there?
Ray!
 Ray who?
Ray-member me?

Knock-Knock!
  Who's there?
Raymond!
  Raymond who?
Raymond me again what I'm doing here!

Knock-Knock!
  Who's there?
Ringo!
  Ringo who?
Ringo round the rosie, pocket full of posie!

Knock-Knock!
  Who's there?
Riot!
  Riot who?
Riot on time, here I am!

Knock-Knock!
  Who's there?
Robin!
  Robin who?
Robin the bank will get you in jail!

Knock-Knock!
  Who's there?
Rockies!
  Rockies who?
Rockies my favorite kind of music!

Knock-Knock!
  Who's there?
Romeo.
  Romeo who?
Romeo-ver to the other side of the river, would ya?

Knock-Knock!
  Who's there?
Ron!
  Ron who?
Ron house! They all look the same!

Knock-Knock!
  Who's there?
Rufus!
  Rufus who?
Rufus falling in!

Knock-Knock!
  Who's there?
Russell.
  Russell who?
Russell me up some grub and I'll tell ya.

Knock-Knock!
  Who's there?
Salami!
  Salami who?
Salami in already!

Knock-Knock!
  Who's there?
Salmon!
  Salmon who?
Salmon chanted evening,
you may meet a stranger!

Knock-Knock!
  Who's there?
Samson!
  Samson who?
Samson you turned out to be! You don't recognize
your own father!

Somebody order
a salami
on rye?

Knock-Knock!
  Who's there?
Sammy!
  Sammy who?
Sammy better directions and I'll get here faster!

Knock-Knock!
  Who's there?
Sandy!
  Sandy who?
Sandy locksmith to get this door open!

Knock-Knock!
  Who's there?
San Francisco!
  San Francisco who?
San Francisco to the store — and tell him to buy
some bread!

Knock-Knock!
  Who's there?
Santa!
  Santa who?
Santa letter, but you never replied!

Knock-Knock!
  Who's there?
Sara!
  Sara who?
Sara-nother time I should come back?

Knock-Knock!
  Who's there?
Sarah!
  Sarah who?
Sarah reason you're not letting me in?

Knock-Knock!
  Who's there?
Scotland!
  Scotland who?
Scotland on his head, we have to take him to the hospital!

Knock-Knock!
  Who's there?
Senior!
  Senior who?
Senior so nosey, I'm not going to tell you who it is!

Knock-Knock!
  Who's there?
Sesame!
  Sesame who?
Sesame out here, now let me in!

Knock-Knock!
  Who's there?
Sheep!
  Sheep who?
Sheep-ritty, don't you think?

Knock-Knock!
  Who's there?
Sheila!
  Sheila who?
Sheila be mad if I don't deliver these flowers!

Knock-Knock!
  Who's there?
Shirley!
  Shirley who?
Shirley you must be joking!

Knock-Knock!
  Who's there?
Shoe!
  Shoe who?
Shoe, kid, ya bother me!

Knock-Knock!
  Who's there?
Shower!
  Shower who?
Shower you care and send flowers!

Knock-Knock!
  Who's there?
Sinker!
  Sinker who?
Sinker swim, it's up to you!

Knock-Knock!
  Who's there?
Simmy!
  Simmy who?
Simmy a get-well card!

Knock-Knock!
  Who's there?
Simon!
  Simon who?
Simon the other side of the door—if you opened it,
you'd know!

Knock-Knock!
  Who's there?
Simon!
  Simon who?
Simon the dotted line and all your troubles will be
over!

Knock-Knock!
  Who's there?
Snow!
  Snow who?
Snow way I'm
waiting out here
— it's freezing!

Knock-Knock!
Who's there?
Soda!
Soda who?
Soda sweater, it's full of holes!

Knock-Knock!
Who's there?
Soldier!
Soldier who?
Soldier comics yet?

Knock-Knock!
Who's there?
Sonata!
Sonata who?
Sonata-s bad as everybody says!

Knock-Knock!
Who's there?
Soup!
Soup who?
Soup-erman to the rescue!

Knock-Knock!
Who's there?
Spain!
Spain who?
Spain in the butt!

Knock-Knock!
 Who's there?
Sparkle!
 Sparkle who?
Sparkle start a fire if you're not careful!

Knock-Knock!
 Who's there?
Sparrow!
 Sparrow who?
Sparrow little
change, pal?

Knock-Knock!
 Who's there?
Stubborn!
 Stubborn who?
Stubborn your toe sure hurts! Ow!

Knock-Knock!
 Who's there?
Stork!
 Stork who?
Stork up on supplies — I'm staying a while!

Knock-Knock!
 Who's there?
Sunday!
 Sunday who?
Sunday in the future we'll meet in person!

Knock-Knock!
  Who's there?
Stan!
  Stan who?
Stan back — I'm breaking the
door down!

Knock-Knock!
  Who's there?
Sturdy!
  Sturdy who?
Sturdy pot, de soup is
burning!

Knock-Knock!
  Who's there?
Stink heap!
  Stink heap who?
EW!

Knock-Knock!
  Who's there?
Sweden!
  Sweden who?
Sweden sour chicken!

T

Knock-Knock!
  Who's there?
Tailor!
  Tailor who?
Tailor head, your choice!

Knock-Knock!
  Who's there?
Termite!
  Termite who?
Termite be something
wrong with your glasses!

Knock-Knock!
  Who's there?
Tex!
  Tex who?
Tex one to know one!

Knock-Knock!
 Who's there?
Thistle!
 Thistle who?
Thistle be the last time I visit you! Sheesh!

Knock-Knock!
 Who's there?
Tina!
 Tina who?
Tina little bug just bit me right on the nose!

Knock-Knock!
 Who's there?
Tuna!
 Tuna who?
Tuna piano and it sounds better!

Knock-Knock!
   Who's there?
Turnip!
   Turnip who?
Turnip the sound, I can't hear
the music!

Knock-Knock!
   Who's there?
Tyrone!
   Tyrone who?
Tyrone shoes, what am I, your slave?

I'll have the spaghetti, easy on the garlic...

Knock-Knock!
   Who's there?
Tyson!
   Tyson who?
Tyson garlic
around your neck.
It's the vampire!

Knock-Knock!
   Who's there?
Udder!
   Udder who?
Udder foolishness to keep reading these jokes!

Knock-Knock!
   Who's there?
Uphill!
   Uphill who?
Uphill could take your headache away!

Knock-Knock!
   Who's there?
Urinal!
   Urinal who?
Urinal lot of trouble!

Nonsense

Knock-Knock!
  Who's there?
Vaughn!
  Vaughn who?
Vaughn day you'll stop acting so crazy!

Knock-Knock!
  Who's there?
Vanessa!
  Vanessa who?
Vanessa door going to open?

Knock-Knock!
  Who's there?
Violins!
  Violins who?
  Violins is a bad way
    to settle an
    argument!

W

Knock-Knock!
  Who's there?
Wales!
  Wales who?
Wales long as I'm here, why don't we go out?

Knock-Knock!
  Who's there?
Walnut!
  Walnut who?
Walnut too sturdy, don't lean on it!

Knock-Knock!
  Who's there?
Wanda!
  Wanda who?
Wanda what you're doing in there!

Knock-Knock!
  Who's there?
Water!
  Water who?
Water you waiting for? Open up!

Hey, Wayne ... Come back! I was just kidding.

Knock-Knock!
  Who's there?
Wayne!
  Wayne who?
Wayne, wayne go away!
Come again some other
day!

Knock-Knock!
  Who's there?
Weaken!
  Weaken who?
Weaken still be friends!

Knock-Knock!
  Who's there?
Wendy!
  Wendy who?
Wendy you'll remember—until then, forget it!

Knock-Knock!
  Who's there?
Whenever!
  Whenever who?
Whenever body going to stop asking me that?

Knock-Knock!
  Who's there?
Who!
  Who who?
What, are you an owl all of a sudden?

Knock-Knock!
　　Who's there?
Whereof?
　　Whereof who?
Whereof all the flowers gone?

Knock-Knock!
　　Who's there?
Wigwam!
　　Wigwam who?
Wigwam your head when it's cold!

It looks so natural.

Knock-Knock!
　　Who's there?
William!
　　William who?
William make me a sandwich?

Knock-Knock!
  Who's there?
Willy!
  Willy who?
Willy let me on the team or not?

Knock-Knock!
  Who's there?
Wilma!
  Wilma who?
Wilma friends never remember my last name?

Knock-Knock!
  Who's there?
Willow!
  Willow who?
Willow quit it with the knock-knocks already?

Knock-Knock!
  Who's there?
Willow!
  Willow who?
Willow or won't you?

Knock-Knock!
  Who's there?
Window!
  Window who?
Window we leave for school?

Knock-Knock!
  Who's there?
Winston!
  Winston who?
Winston of you guys
threw that paper airplane?

Knock-Knock!
  Who's there?
Wooden!
  Wooden who?
Wooden you rather be playing basketball?

Knock-Knock!
  Who's there?
Woody!
  Woody who?
Woody want, can't you see I'm busy!

Knock-Knock!
  Who's there?
Wylie!
  Wylie who?
Wylie answers the door, the house is burning down!

Knock-Knock!
  Who's there?
X.R.!
  X.R. who?
X.R. great with bacon!

Y

Knock-Knock!
  Who's there?
Yachts!
  Yachts who?
Yachts a very good question!

Knock-Knock!
  Who's there?
Yam!
  Yam who?
Yam what I am!

Knock-Knock!
  Who's there?
Yee!
  Yee who?
Hey, are you a cowboy or
what?

Knock-Knock!
   Who's there?
Yoda!
   Yoda who?
Yoda one who wants to know, so why don't you guess!

Knock-Knock!
   Who's there?
You!
   You who?
Yes, how can I help you?

Knock-Knock!
   Who's there?
Yugo!
   Yugo who?
Yugo first, I'll be right behind ya!

Knock-Knock!
   Who's there?
Yuri!
   Yuri who?
Yuri up and open the door!

Knock-Knock!
  Who's there?
Zany!
  Zany who?
Zany way to get you to stop with the knock-knocks?

Knock-Knock!
  Who's there?
Zoe!
  Zoe who?
Zoe doesn't recognize
my voice now?

Knock-Knock!
  Who's there?
Enzo Z.!
  Enzo Z. who?
Enzo Z. knock-knock
book!

I thought it would never end!

Index

Ants, 6
Aspirin, 59
Bacon, 92
Baseball, 48
Basketball, 91
Bath time, 12
Batman, 42
Bird, 32
Birthday, 4
Books, 16
Boss, 13, 64
Brother, twin, 37
Bug, 83
Bull, 9, 13, 22
Burp, 34
Bus, 10
Cake, take the, 29
Candy, 55
Cans, 50
Car, 16, 17, 20
Card, getwell, 78
Cat, 17, 33, 35
Champ, 39
Chasing, 47
Chicken, sweet and
  sour, 81
Christmas, 48
Closet, 67
Clothes, 19, 64
Cold, 20, 28
Comb, 40
Cook, 20
Cookies, 12
Coughing, 20
Cow, 61, 85; interrupt-
  ing, 45
Cowboy, 93
Crow, 59
Crying, 30
Cuckoo, 20
Dark, 35
Dessert, 45
Dinner, 45, 53
Dog, 32, 33, 44
Door, 57, 67, 78, 81, 86
Doorbell, 27, 45, 51
Dress, 26
Easter eggs, 13
Evening, some enchant-
  ed, 74
Father, 74
Fire, 80

Fish, 24, 33
Flower, 17, 68, 77, 89
Fly, 28
Food, 20
Foot, 58
Football, 25
France, 34
Friend, old, 7
Friends, 43, 52, 88, 90
Frisbee, 52
Garlic, 84
Gas tank, 68
Glasses, 40, 82
Gloves, 39
Grass, 60
Gravy, 66
Grilled cheese, 38
Gun, squirt, 15
Hands, 40
Headache, 59, 85
Heads or tails, 82
Homework, 44, 51
Horns, 22
Hospital, 76
House, 26, 91
Hunger, 5, 13
Idea, 39
Jail, 72
Job, 54
Jokes, 49, 59, 85
Key, 19, 34, 42
Kiss, 37, 48, 61, 70
Knock-knock jokes, 5,
  13, 20, 25, 32, 35,
  41, 43, 55, 70, 90,
  95; book, 24, 95
Lawn, 27, 60
Leg, 66
Letter, 75
Lies, 55, 65
Loans, 11, 15
Locksmith, 75
Love, 15, 17, 56
Magazines, 44
Manual, 29
Maple syrup, 56
Marriage, 56
Matador, 9
Math, 58
Money, 18
Morse code, 60
Music, 73, 84

Nap, 53
Needle, 3
Opera, 54
Owl, 88
Paint. 4
Pants, 66
Paper airplane, 91
Pears, 66
Penny, 69
Phone, 39, 65
Piano, 84
Pizza, 34, 49, 69
Punch line, 21
Question, 93; silly, 18,
  53
Rain, 14, 30, 54, 64, 88
Reindeer, 71
Roof, 73
Sandwich, 49, 89
School, 12, 23, 26, 30,
  42, 90
Seashells, 18
Sheep, 76
Shoes, 84
Skateboard, 31
Sneeze, 67
Snowman, 39
Soup, 81
Summer, 38
Superman, 79
Supplies, 80
Sweater, 79
Teacher, 30
Team, 90
Television, 52
Tennis, 25
Thief, 48
Tickets, 57
Toe, 80
Tooth, 3
Train, 58
Trouble, 85
Tuna, 50
Turban, 71
Upstairs, 51
Vampire, 84
Voice, 19, 95
Waffles, 56
Wedding, 16
Yelling, 23

"How do I find my target customers? How can I stand out in this crazy new complex marketplace? These are the questions facing every entrepreneur today. The challenge of navigating this new world of blogs, tweets, and Facebook requires expertise and strategy that few of us have. That's why Patricia Vaccarino and her *pr for people* has become an invaluable, effective resource for business owners and service providers. She has been a leader in adapting old school fundamentals of branding, marketing, and PR to this new universe of Web 2.0. She's a master at helping you reach your target market and standing out in cyberspace. I've worked with Patricia and have seen firsthand how she spots trends and positions her clients exactly where they need to be at exactly the right time. Working with Patricia is the best investment you can make in your business."

&. Lorraine Howell

Author of *Give Your Elevator Speech a Lift!*

Owner, Media Skills Training

Seattle, WA

"Patricia Vaccarino's vast experience in PR guides us through why what used to work no longer does, and she takes what can be a daunting subject to some and makes it user-friendly and immediately usable."

&. Mary Key, Ph.D.

Leadership Expert

Author of *CEO Road Rules*

Tampa, FL

"Good work alone is not enough to propel a career and standard PR efforts aren't enough to get past all the clutter. Patricia's insights and 'how-to' advice can guide executives and entrepreneurs alike to create and execute a truly powerful PR strategy that will enhance their careers for years to come."

&. Kurt Weyerhauser

Managing Partner, Kensington-Stone

Los Angeles, CA

"Patricia Vaccarino is my favorite PR professional—not just because she has years in the business, or the fact that she's well-connected, or incredibly skilled at getting meaningful awareness. It's because she is as equally skilled at using these traits to promote professionals as well as her corporate clients. Patricia brings her skills in reputation and promotional management to the practice of professional branding, resulting in a must-read book for any professional wanting to maximize their success and increase their opportunities."

&ะ Eric Weaver
DDB Advertising
Vancouver, B.C.

"As a journalist I have spent countless hours over the past 25 years searching for the right expert sources. In this book Patricia Vaccarino does more than tell people how they can become an expert but creates a roadmap for getting journalists to interview them. *PR for People* is not just a boon for those who want to be known as the go-to sources but is making my job easier, because when experts make themselves memorable they become easier for me to find."

&ะ Manny Frishberg
Journalist
Seattle, WA

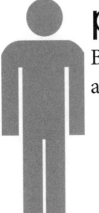

pr for people

Be famous for who you are
and what you do.

PATRICIA VACCARINO

BOOK PUBLISHERS NETWORK

Book Publishers Network
P.O. Box 2256
Bothell • WA • 98041
PH • 425-483-3040
www.bookpublishersnetwork.com

10 9 8 7 6 5 4 3 2 1

Printed in the United States of America

LCCN 2009910503
ISBN10 1-935359-23-1
ISBN13 978-1-935359-23-4

Editor: Vicki McCown
Cover Designer: Nina Barnett
Typographer: Stephanie Martindale